HOW STEM BUILT EMPIRES™

HOW STEM BUILT THE AZTEC EMPIRE

AMIE JANE LEAVITT

Published in 2020 by The Rosen Publishing Group, Inc.
29 East 21st Street, New York, NY 10010

First Edition

Library of Congress Cataloging-in-Publication Data

Names: Leavitt, Amie Jane, author.
Title: How STEM built the Aztec Empire / Amie Jane Leavitt.
Description: First edition. | New York : Rosen Publishing, 2020. | Series: How STEM built empires | Audience: Grades: 7 to 12. | Includes bibliographical references and index.
Identifiers: LCCN 2019008454| ISBN 9781725341357 (library bound) | ISBN 9781725341340 (pbk.)
Subjects: LCSH: Science—Mexico—Mexico City—History—To 1500—Juvenile literature. | Aztecs—Mexico—Mexico City—History—Juvenile literature. | Technology—Mexico—Mexico City—History—To 1500—Juvenile literature. | Engineering—Mexico—Mexico City—History—To 1500—Juvenile literature. | Mathematics—Mexico—Mexico City—History—To 1500—Juvenile literature.
Classification: LCC Q127.M4 L43 2020 | DDC 303.48/30972530902—dc23
LC record available at https://lccn.loc.gov/2019008454

Manufactured in the United States of America

On the cover: One of the empire's most iconic artifacts, the Aztec Sun Stone is displayed in Mexico City.

CONTENTS

INTRODUCTION

The year was 1978 and a team of utility workers had just finished digging in the center of Mexico City. Not too far underneath the city streets, they uncovered something unexpected: a massive monolith.

After dusting off the stone artwork, they discovered odd carvings on it. The relief showed the image of a woman with small bells by her face. She was not wearing any clothing and her body was dismembered and decapitated. The image was likely strange to those who did not know what it represented, but Aztec experts knew exactly whom it portrayed: the famous Aztec moon goddess Coyolxauhqui, whose name means "bells on her face." This goddess was strongly connected to the Aztec's most important pyramid, the Templo Mayor—or Great Temple—through one of the culture's most noted legends.

Most of the Great Temple had been dismantled by the Spanish conquistadores when they conquered the Aztec capital of Tenochtitlán in 1521. The massive stones from the temple had been used to construct the cathedral and other important colonial structures in Mexico City. However, the foundations and lower parts of the temple had always been suspected to be somewhere nearby. Now, this monolith revealed the precise location of its base.

This circular stone monolith represents an Aztec legend about Coyolxauhqui, the Aztec moon goddess. It was found in Mexico City in 1978 and has become a symbol of the Aztec empire.

Because of the important nature of this discovery, the Mexican president, José López Portillo, immediately demanded that all utility and construction work stop in the area. Archaeologists rushed to the scene with tools in hand; they were charged by the president to uncover whatever they could of the ancient temple. Teams of archaeologists, under the lead of Eduardo Matos Montezuma, went right to work.

During the decades since the original discovery, large sections of the Templo Mayor and thousands of artifacts have been uncovered in the heart of Mexico City. As the archaeologists have dug deeper over the years, they have been able to peel back the layers of time and determine that the temple was not built all at once, but rather over many generations. The first temple was constructed in the early 1400s and the last was constructed sometime in the first decade of the 1500s. As subsequent generations decided to improve or enlarge the temple, they just built a brand-new temple right on top of and around the old one. This gave the new structure a larger footprint and a higher rise than the previous structures.

The archaeological evidence of Tenochtitlán is not only impressive from a historical perspective, it is also remarkable from a STEM (science, technology, engineering, and mathematics) standpoint. After all, it reveals one overwhelming fact about the Aztec builders: they were part of a highly advanced civilization that utilized countless STEM practices in the construction of their metropolis. This fact is made evident by the impressive structures, artwork, and artifacts that this long-lost people left behind deep underneath present-day Mexico City. The advanced STEM skills used to build one of the grandest cities in the world is an amazing achievement considering that the Aztec society existed more than five hundred years ago.

CHAPTER ONE

BIRTH OF AN EMPIRE

When Hernán Cortés and his men arrived in the New World in 1519, the Aztecs controlled the bulk of 80,000 square miles (207,000 square kilometers) that makes up present-day central Mexico. The reach of Aztec society stretched from the Gulf of Mexico in the east to the Pacific Ocean in the west and from the northern and southern borders of present-day Mexico.

This truly was the height of the Aztec Empire, with a gleaming, organized capital city, a highly developed public works system, and an efficient agricultural structure. It also had a sizeable population. Keep in mind that the largest city in Spain at that time was Seville, which had a population of about 30,000. The city of Tenochtitlán had an estimated 200,000 to 250,000 inhabitants, making it the third-largest city in the world at that time, behind Constantinople (present-day Istanbul), Turkey, and Paris, France. The overall Aztec Empire included about 5 million people.

FROM SIMPLE BEGINNINGS TO MYSTIC VISIONS

However, the Aztecs had not always been a major force in Mesoamerica. Their beginnings were much

This manuscript page is from Diego Duran's book *History of Indians.* This illustration shows Cortés arriving on horseback and being welcomed by the Aztecs.

simpler. Historians believe that the Aztecs (who called themselves the Mexica) were most likely a nomadic tribe of hunter-gatherers from the deserts of northern Mexico. According to Aztec legends, they hailed from a place called Aztlan, meaning the "White Land," and arrived in the more fertile lands of Mesoamerica sometime around the early thirteenth century. They were not the first people to dwell in this land—there were many tribes of peoples already living here in small tribal communities and city-states. There were also many deserted cities lying in ruins leftover from ancient civilizations.

AZTEC RECORDS

Most of Aztec history was passed down in oral traditions in the Aztec's native language: Nahuatl. However, they did also have a collection of records that were written in ideographs. When the Spanish conquered the Aztecs in 1521, though, the conquistadores destroyed many of the Aztec records because they felt that they contained heretical teachings.

In the decades that followed this conquest, Spanish leaders tasked the Aztec priests and artisans with creating a series of codices that documented important information about their empire. There are about five hundred of these tomes in existence today, and they are known as the Aztec codices. Some of the most noted works include the *Codex Mendoza*, *Florentine Codex*, *Codex Vergara*, and the *Santa María Asunción*. They document the history of the Aztec civilization, chronicle the daily life of the people, tell about the wars fought and the exact tributes paid by subjects, and detail specific data about landholdings and taxes. Much of what is known about the Aztecs today comes from a combination of sources: the Aztec codices, the firsthand accounts of the Spaniards, and the archaeological evidence that is still being uncovered at dig sites in Mexico City.

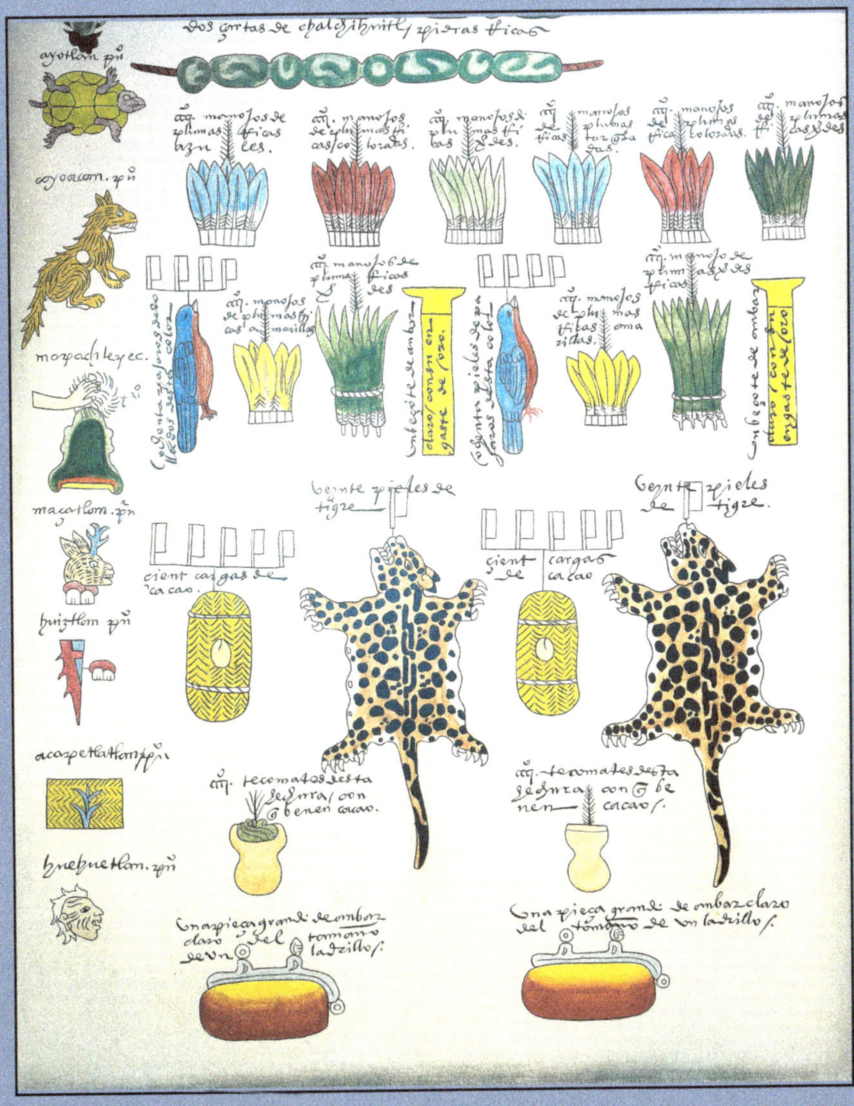

This is a reproduction of a page from the *Codex Mendoza*. It shows some examples of the taxes that were paid to the Aztec rulers by their subjects.

Around 1325, as legend has it, the Aztecs decided that it was in their best interest to form an alliance with one of the tribes in the area. To do so, one of the young Aztec men would marry the daughter of the tribal king. On the eve of her wedding, the Aztec noblemen took her to the top of an ancient temple. They then sacrificed her to their god of fertility. When the king found out about the death of his daughter, he was devastated—and furious. First, the alliance between the two tribes was off. He and his forces chased after the Aztecs in retaliation for the brutal murder of the princess. The Aztecs fled by boats onto a large nearby lake—Lake Texcoco—and then onto an island, where they sought refuge. This marshy island, which was barely inhabitable when the Aztecs first arrived, would eventually become the great capital city of Tenochtitlán. Their city was named after Tenoch, the religious leader of the Aztecs from approximately 1325 to 1370.

Aztec legend claims that when the people first came to this marshy island in Lake Texcoco, their leader—Tenoch—saw a vision of a prickly pear cactus growing on a rock in the middle of the lake. In his vision, an eagle swoops down and sits on top of the cactus, clutching a serpent in its beak.

The vision was filled with symbolism for the Aztecs. First, their religion taught that the cactus grew out of the heart of one of their goddesses, Copil, who was the sister of their war and sun god, Huitzilopochtli. Since the cactus was growing out of a rock on the island, they believed that this important goddess

Mexico's modern flag proudly displays an eagle gripping a snake while it rests on a cactus, which is part of one of the Aztecs' most significant legends.

must therefore dwell on the island, symbolizing good fortune. As a result, the people saw this vision as a sign from the gods. It was simple: this swampy land, even though it did not have the most ideal conditions, was to be their new home. On the modern-day Mexican flag, at the center of the ensign is an image of an eagle clutching a serpent while sitting on a prickly pear cactus—a reference to the vision of Tenoch.

AZTEC RULERS

During its nearly two hundred year history, the Aztec people were ruled by a religious leader followed by ten kings. Their reigns were as follows:

- **1325–1370** Tenoch (religious ruler)
- **1376–1395** Acamapichtli (first king)
- **1395–1417** Huitzilihuitl
- **1417–1427** Chimalpopoca
- **1427–1440** Itzcoatl
- **1440–1469** Montezuma I
- **1469–1481** Azayactl
- **1481–1486** Tizoc
- **1486–1502** Ahuitzotl
- **1502–1520** Montezuma II
- **1520–1521** Cuitlahuac

IN SEARCH OF INSPIRATION

The Aztecs dreamed of building a grand city on their island that was modeled after one of the nearby deserted cities, known as Teotihuacán. This city was believed to be the city of the gods and, according to local folklore, was the birthplace of the sun. The ruins of the ancient civilization included a grand temple known as the Pyramid of the Sun. The temple was huge, with a base about the same size as Egypt's Great Pyramid of Giza and about 1 million cubic yards (764,554 cubic meters) of earth and soil. The layout of the city—as far as the Aztecs were concerned—had been dictated by the gods themselves. Therefore, to appease the gods, they wanted to re-create a city just like this one on their boggy island. Despite high hopes, it would take many generations for this dream to actually become reality.

Under the reign of the Aztec's first king, Acamapichtli (1376–1395), the Aztecs began laying out the plans for their own great city. However, they had to battle many natural elements working against them—water being the main obstacle. The Aztecs quickly realized the challenges that came with trying to build anything on the marshy island. The ground was unstable, and anything of weight would either topple or sink into the ground. Their solution to this problem was STEM genius. To make a solid foundation, the Aztec engineers used a wooden piling system. Workers cut 30-foot-long (9.1-meter) stakes that were 3 to 4 inches (7.6 to 10.2 centimeters) wide. They then pounded these stakes deep into the ground and filled in the gaps between the stakes with volcanic stone. These wooden pilings created a stable foundation on which they could safely build massive, heavy structures, including pyramids, palaces, causeways, and bridges.

Experts estimate that it took about one hundred years for the Aztecs to become a full-fledged empire. During that one hundred years—as far as military and cultural power was concerned—they were a fairly insignificant group of people. They spent most of their time building up their city and forming alliances with neighboring tribes. In 1428, the Aztecs joined up with two other city-states. This triple alliance of people from Tenochtitlán, Texcoco, and Tlacopan tribes became what is called today the Aztec Empire. The empire lasted for nearly a century, until the Spanish conquered the Aztecs in 1521.

CHAPTER TWO

SURROUNDED BY WATER

In addition to the Aztec's island home being unsuited to grand construction, it also lacked easy access to clean drinking water. Yes, there was water all around Tenochtitlán, but it was a false hope. The water of Lake Texcoco was salty (since there was no river outlet from the lake) and therefore not drinkable. There was, however, crystal-clear spring water available on the nearby mainland. At first, the people just canoed back and forth from the island to the spring and brought water back in jugs and other types of pottery. However, this method of water supply was not sustainable, especially as the population grew in size. It was simply not practical to retrieve water in such a fashion on a large scale. So what did they do? In the early 1400s, the Aztecs became one of the few civilizations in the world to build an aqueduct system. An aqueduct is an artificial channel or canal that is used for water transport. Aqueducts can either be above ground, in the form of a bridge, or underground, in the form of a tunnel. The Aztecs needed to move clean water over a lake, so their aqueduct was elevated.

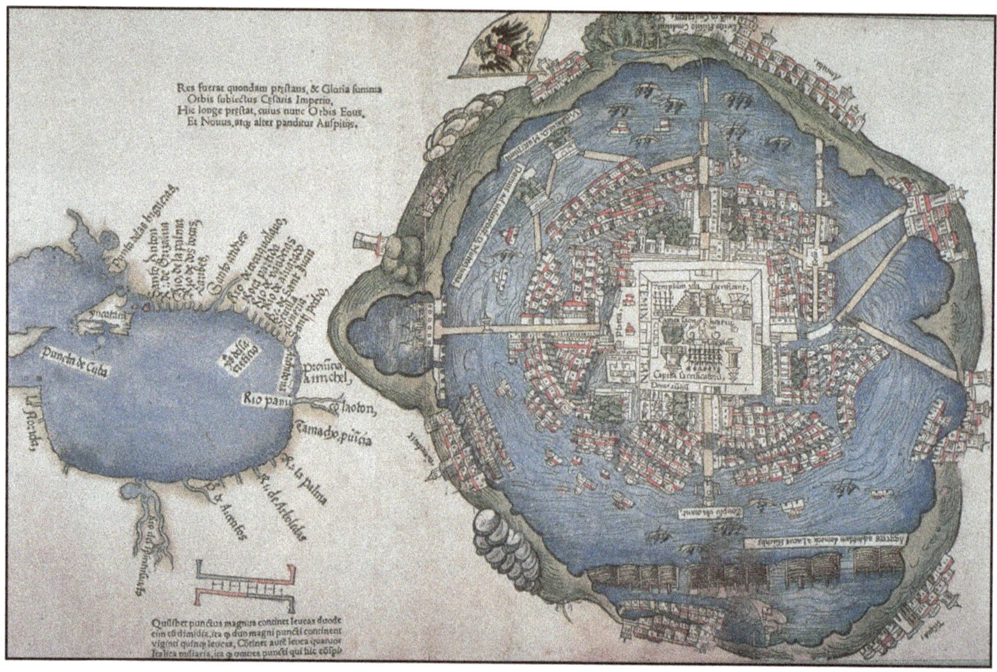

This aerial view of Tenochtitlán displays the city's unique location and the adaptations used by the Aztecs to make a city in the middle of a lake one of the largest, most-populated cities in the world.

THE FIRST AQUEDUCTS

Historians believe that the Aztecs began the construction of their first aqueduct in the year 1418, during the reign of Chimalpopoca. To construct this aqueduct, the Aztecs first had to build a system of artificial islands that were about 10 to 13 feet (3 to 4 m) apart and spanned the lake from the mainland to Tenochtitlán. To build these islands, they again turned to STEM. Just as they did to stabilize their island home, Aztec engineers drove thousands of

CANOEING ABOUT

Since the capital city of Tenochtitlán was surrounded by water, the Aztecs often used canoes to transport people and goods from place to place. When the Spanish arrived, the lakes were filled with as many as two hundred thousand canoes. These canoes came in a variety of sizes, including small, one-man crafts and massive vessels that could either carry dozens of people or supplies weighing up to 3 tons (2.7 metric tons). These large canoes were made out of giant spruce trees and were about 50 feet (15.2 m) in length. It is assumed that because of the Aztecs' geographical location on an island, they would have used canoes from the very beginning of their civilization. They would have improved them to suit their needs over the centuries. Accordingly, canoes are pictured in many of the Aztec codices, including the *Codex Mendoza.*

wooden pilings into the lake bed and then constructed a flat surface on top. Once the foundation of these miniature islands was secure, the second step was to build mud mounds on top of each. As they built these, the Aztecs again utilized a system of wooden pilings to provide stability for the mound and keep its soil in place. The tops of the mounds were then carved out to form a single trough, which was then lined with clay. The usage of clay was important, as it is an impermeable soil that would prevent water leakage in the canal. These troughs on the small islands were then connected to each other through a series of extended hollowed-out logs. Thus, when the earthwork and wooden canals were finished, there was a man-made elevated ditch that extended all the way from the Chapultepec spring on the mainland to the people who lived in Tenochtitlán.

This first aqueduct system was effective, bringing clean drinking water right to the heart of Tenochtitlán. The water was then spread throughout the city by a series of canals, or hand-delivered in jugs or canoes. Unfortunately, however, this did not last long. The aqueduct was destroyed in a massive flood in 1449. As is the case with any engineering failure, the engineers learned from what worked and what did not work in the original aqueduct. This allowed them to make improvements to the design as they implemented their second system.

The second aqueduct was constructed in the same area as the original, beginning in the 1450s. However, Aztec engineers knew that since repeated flooding from the lake was definitely a possibility, they should elevate this new canal higher than the last one. In addition, the second aqueduct would not be made of earth and wood. This one would be constructed of masonry for increased strength and durability. Another design change—which was probably the most impressive—was that the new aqueduct was a twin-tube construction as opposed to the single culvert of most aqueducts, including their original design.

The Aztecs had figured out that it was best to have a dual-channel system. That way, they would always have fresh water flowing to the city and would not have to stop the flow if they needed to clean or repair the channel. If one channel was blocked or needed to be closed for maintenance, the other could still bring in a flow of crucial water. This dual-channel aqueduct was an ambitious engineering project that would have required expert science, mathematics, and engineering knowledge—as well as a large labor force. The canal was 5 feet (1.5 m) high and 3 feet (.9 m) wide and stretched for 3 miles (4.8 km). In Tenochtitlán, the water from the aqueduct bubbled into public fountains and filled reservoirs. The aqueduct even filled special stone bathtubs built for the king, who bathed twice a day.

AMERICA'S LARGEST EARTHWORKS PROJECT

Another significant problem faced by the Aztecs—and their building projects—was the threat of floods. The lakes around them were spring fed and had no outlets, such as rivers or streams. Consequently, in seasons with heavy rainfall, the lakes would rise and flood Tenochtitlán. The flood in the mid-1400s that destroyed the first aqueduct nearly destroyed

Montezuma I, depicted here, was responsible for one noteworthy Aztec STEM project: the conception and construction of an enormous series of dikes to protect Tenochtitlán from flooding.

the whole island capital. The flooding would also frequently damage the region's freshwater lakes, which were located to the south of Tenochtitlán. When saltwater from the salty lakes poured into their freshwater system, the increase in salinity would harm the wildlife and ecosystem of these lakes.

During the reign of Montezuma I in the mid-fifteenth century, Aztec engineers designed a solution to this problem. They constructed a massive wall, or dike, just east of the city. It extended 10 miles (16 km) across the lake and was intended to hold back the water and protect the city from floods. Since the lake was shallow, the wall had to be only 12 feet (3.6 m) high. However, to keep out the water, it was 27 feet (8 m) wide. The dike was constructed from sticks, reeds, stone, and earth. Throughout the wicker wall, there were sluice gates—which would have likely been just wooden doors—that could be raised or lowered to control the water level behind the dike. This dike did not just protect the city—it also prevented the salt water in the north from infiltrating the freshwater in the southern part of the lake. Experts believe that this safe zone, which was constructed to protect the city, was the largest earthworks project in the Americas at that time.

CHAPTER THREE

BUILDING A CITY

Tenochtitlán was modeled after the ancient city of Teotihuacán. Inspired by its orderly planning and impressive constructions, Aztec planners wanted to develop their grand city to mimic Teotihuacán's amazing architectural achievements. Tenochtitlán was divided into four gridded quadrants that radiated out from a central area called the Sacred Precinct. Inside this special zone stood all of the city's most important structures, including pyramid temples, palaces, mansions, ball courts, and a great market square. The market attracted some sixty thousand people a day to buy and sell food, jewels, gold, silver, precious stones, feathers, shells, and other goods. There were an estimated seventy-eight structures in the precinct, and they were all constructed out of massive blocks of stone.

ACCESS TO THE CITY

One might ask: how on earth did this group of people—without modern technology—transport such enormous, heavy blocks to a swampy island in the center of a lake? The answer lies in the engineering genius of causeways. These large, over-water roadways were constructed to connect Tenochtitlán to the mainland. It is believed that the first causeway was constructed around 1350. Eventually, there were three causeways that connected Tenochtitlán to the mainland.

To build these roads, the Aztecs used their trusty wood piling system to drive two parallel lines of stakes into the lake bed. They then filled the spaces between the pilings with stone and soil. Unlike in other Aztec construction projects, the causeway pilings needed to stick out above the water level so that the eventual roadway itself would not be submerged in the lake when it was added later.

According to Frances Berdan, an archaeologist specializing in Aztec culture, "These causeways were built very straight and wide with [draw]bridges that would open up and connect the city to the north, to the west, and to the south." The drawbridges served two purposes. First, they allowed canoes to move easily on all parts of the lake. When a canoe approached the drawbridge, it could lift up and let the canoe pass. Second, the drawbridges served as protection for the city. If the city were being attacked, officials could lift the drawbridges and the enemy would no longer be able to invade via the causeways.

HUMAN POWER

Once the causeways were constructed, the Aztecs had a clear path to transporting large blocks of stone from quarries to the capital. However, it still would have been challenging for the Aztecs to do so. There is no evidence that this group of people had access to beasts of burden—draft animals such as donkeys, mules, llamas, camels, horses, or oxen—to carry or pull the weighty stone blocks. As such, it is likely that they had to haul these stones using human power. Historians have estimated that it took tens of thousands of laborers to move a single stone block from a quarry—around 25 miles (40.2 km) south of Tenochtitlán—to a temple pyramid. To aid in the transportation of this heavy load, they used logs as rollers underneath the supersized blocks. These logs would slowly spin as the stone blocks were dragged over them, thus reducing the total amount of force required by the workers.

Because of the pyramid temples' religious significance, the Aztecs considered them to be their most important construction projects. To Mesoamericans, pyramids represented mountains—the highest and nearest places to heaven. They were believed to be the homes of their gods and their ancestors. In fact, in Nahuatl, pyramid temples are called *teocalli*, or "god houses." Pyramid temples always faced west and were located on the eastern side of the towns' central plazas.

Despite being commonly called pyramids, these structures are more accurately ziggurats because they have flat tops. This is different from Egyptian pyramids, which rise to an apex point. The flat top allows a temple—or temples—to be constructed at the top of the ziggurat. The flat top is also an invitation—these structures are meant to be climbed so that people could worship the gods on top of them.

This illustration shows the flat-top design of most Aztec temples. These temples were often the sites of massive religious ceremonies, such as the one depicted here at the foot of the Templo Mayor.

The Templo Mayor in Tenochtitlán was the first major structure built by the Aztecs in their island city. The first version of this temple was finished in 1390. Then, larger temples were constructed over the top of this one until the final one was dedicated in 1487. The final temple was the largest structure in the city. It was a twin-stair pyramid, meaning it had two sets of steep staircases leading to the top. The base measured

MILITARY MIGHT

According to historian Manuel Aguilar-Moreno, one reason that the Aztecs built their capital city at such a grand scale was to showcase their military strength. The Aztecs were not happy only to rule the land now known as the Valley of Mexico, where Tenochtitlán was located. Rather, they were constantly engaging in warfare—conquering other civilizations—until their empire stretched from sea to sea. They were an aggressive society, a powerful society, and a motivated society. As a result of these conquests, everyone in the subjugated lands had to pay significant tributes to the Aztecs. These tributes helped the city of Tenochtitlán grow in wealth and power. Examples of the tributes demanded by the Aztecs include such items as cotton, clothing, shields, feathers, warrior costumes, precious metals and gemstones, and food items.

1,200 feet (365 m) on each side of the square and was completely surrounded by a stone wall. It rose some 200 feet (60 m) tall—which is roughly half the height of the Pyramid of Giza. At the top of the Great Temple stood two shrines. One was for the Aztec god Huitzilopochtli—the god of war and the sun—and the other was for Tlaloc—the god of rain. This double temple teocalli was unique to Aztec architecture, and it was the most impressive structure in an already impressive city.

LET'S PLAY BALL!

By tradition, the first thing that the Aztecs did when they settled a new location was build a shrine to their primary god, Huitzilopochtli. The very next thing they built was a ball court. This game represented an important legend about Huitzilopochtli, which they considered sacred.

These ball courts were built with a grass or soil playing area surrounded by sloping stone walls. The court was in the shape of an *I*, with end zones that were either open or enclosed by stone walls. On each side wall, a stone ring was often attached. It is believed that part of the game involved throwing a rubber ball through the ring. There were many variations on the rules of the game, including differences in scoring and the rules of conduct.

Surprisingly, the Aztecs did have rubber balls for playing. In fact, Mesoamericans were among the first civilizations to come up with a way to use

Ball games similar to the one shown here were played not just by the Aztecs, but by countless other Mesoamerican tribes and civilizations.

natural latex. Once they harvested the latex from the rubber trees, they would mix it with the juice from morning glory vines. Aztec chemists would have had to experiment with different percentages of each ingredient to find the ideal recipe since different quantities would produce rubber that was either too bouncy or too brittle. Not only did the Aztecs make balls out of rubber, they also made sandals.

LIVING IN THE LAP OF LUXURY

Next to the Templo Mayor in Tenochtitlán stood the king's residence, a palace where hundreds of nobles and courtiers lived and worked. In addition to the thousands of nobles on the palace grounds daily, servants were also present in large numbers. It is estimated that about three thousand people tended to the needs of the king and the palace. They took care of the grounds, cleaned the rooms, cooked the food, guarded the palace, and tended to the animals in the aviary and zoo. The king's palace was an enormous stone structure about 540,000 square feet (50,000 sq m) in size. It had hundreds of rooms, about one hundred baths, a spacious courtyard, patios, gardens, ponds, and even a ten-room aviary and zoo with such exotic animals as eagles, pumas, and jaguars.

Many common people's homes had access to nearby baths as well. The Aztecs knew the value of personal hygiene—and many bathed multiple times each day. The Aztec hothouses were igloo shaped; one wall would be heated from a fire on the outside, then the people inside the sauna would throw water on the wall, which would create steam for the bathhouse. In addition to building saunas, the people also utilized their scientific knowledge of local plants to make natural soaps to clean both their bodies and their clothing on a regular basis. They also used plants for deodorants and as toothpaste, making the Aztecs one of the most hygienic societies in the world.

CHAPTER FOUR

ADVANCEMENTS IN AGRICULTURE

The problem of getting drinkable water into Tenochtitlán was solved early on in the settlement of the island city. However, the population of Tenochtitlán still had to be fed. Unfortunately, there was little farmable land on the marshy islands on Lake Texcoco. One solution the Aztecs utilized was to construct special floating farms called chinampas. No one knows for sure who invented the chinampa system, but the historical consensus is that it was used throughout Mesoamerica for hundreds of years prior to the rise of the Aztec Empire. However, experts believe that the Aztecs were the first to use this agricultural system on a mass scale, which they did to support the population of an enormous city.

CHINAMPA CONSTRUCTION

First of all, it is important to understand that even though chinampas looked like they were floating islands, they actually were not. They were a form of wetland or raised field cultivation. These small, island-based agricultural mounds were built in one of two ways.

One method was to tame swampy areas of land. Farmers would go to a soggy area and begin digging ditches all the way around the perimeter of a rectangular section. As they dug, the farmers piled the mud from the ditches onto the rectangular plot. This elevated the plot higher and higher above the ditches. As the farmer dug deeper, the ditches would eventually fill in with water because of the marshy land's high water level. Once that happened, the rectangular piece of land had been transformed into a chinampa. He would then repeat this process on other plots of land parallel to the first one. By leaving the ditches of water in between, he could access the entire array of chinampas by canoe.

The second way farmers would build a chinampa was by raising a field from the lake bed. First, farmers would test the water depth in an area along the lakeshore with a long pole. Once they found a shallow area, they would pound strong reeds into the lake bed to form a rectangle. They would often use some kind of latticework as a fence around this perimeter, which would hold the mud they were about to pile up. Once they had their reed and lattice framework, the farmers would dig into the lake bed on the outside of this perimeter of the reeds, heaping mud from the lake bed in between the reeds. They would bring in mats of vegetation to layer on top of the growing mud pile. They kept on layering mud and vegetation until the mound was well above water level.

Once the chinampas were formed, the farmers would then plant willow trees around the perimeter of the plots. These trees served several purposes. Their

Chinampas still exist in the Valley of Mexico, such as these "islands" that demonstrate the second type of chinampa construction method.

deep roots helped to stabilize the newly formed land; they served as a barrier to erosion and wind damage; and they helped protect the plot from the effects of frost on cold days by trapping warm air under their canopy. This increased the growing season on the chinampas and was one of the reasons why Aztec farmers were able to harvest several times each year. Even by modern standards, this is remarkable, as the growing pattern for many important crops prevents repeated annual harvesting.

The chinampas created an ideal environment for plant growth. Farmers never had to worry about watering their crops—the water that surrounded the chinampas provided a constant water source for the plants' roots. Since fish and other marine life lived in the waters that surrounded the chinampas, the water was fairly nutrient rich as well because of the presence of animal waste products in the water. Therefore, the plants were able to receive some of the nutrients they needed just from their water source.

Regardless of the construction method, the advanced STEM behind these chinampas was undeniable. Though farmers may not have known the exact science behind the chinampa structure, they were still able to figure out the necessary conditions for mixing lake mud, fertile soil, and resilient seeds to make these agricultural islands function. The engineering behind a chinampa also demonstrated an impressive understanding of structural integrity and drainage pathways.

THE POWER OF FARMING

Some have argued that the chinampa system was one of humankind's most productive agricultural systems. On these floating gardens, the Aztecs grew all kinds of crops, including corn, squash, and beans. The chinampas allowed the Aztecs of Tenochtitlán to be a self-sufficient people. They grew enough food on the chinampas to feed not only their own population in the city, but also the population of the surrounding area. It is estimated that about two million people were fed by the expansive Aztec chinampa system. Experts believe that it was this advanced form of agriculture that allowed the Aztecs to become such a dominant force in the region, as keeping the population fed was a struggle for all ancient civilizations.

The land in Tenochtitlán was quite flat, but the mainland around the lake was more mountainous. In the hilly regions of the Aztec Empire, the people had their own struggles finding land to farm. In these areas, they would often resort to terrace farming.

Terrace farming methods were used by the Aztecs and other ancient Mesoamericans. Though the Aztecs did not invent this method, they certainly benefited from it.

Using this method of agriculture, farmers would build stone walls on hillsides. Then, they would fill up the space between the wall and the sloped hillside with soil. This would create a flat area of land that could be used to grow crops. The farmer would continue to build these walls higher up the slope until the entire hillside had been transformed into farmable land.

The Aztecs utilized three different methods to keep soil fertile. First, they practiced crop rotation. Second, they often planted the "three sisters" at the same time: maize, squash, and beans. These plants were soil friendly and helped keep the earth rich in nutrients. Third, they sometimes let their land take a rest and did not plant anything on it for a length of time.

Another way the Aztecs took care of their land was by providing it with nutrients. Human and animal waste was collected from the capital city. Then, it was canoed to the chinampas or hauled to the terraced farms and spread out on the land. These natural fertilizers helped add nitrogen back to the depleted soil.

PLANT EXPERTS

When the Spanish showed up in the New World, the Aztecs had already spent decades cultivating their knowledge of crops, flowers, and medicinal foliage. As a result, they used about three thousand different types of medicinal herbs for many kinds of ailments.

BOTANICAL GARDENS

The Aztecs had beautiful botanical gardens. In these gardens, they designed and built a variety of water features, including irrigation pipes, aqueducts, pools, and waterfalls. A wide variety of plants grew here, including vanilla orchid, cacao trees, foodstuff plants, and medicinal plants and herbs. Reproduced in Ian Mursell's Mexicolore.com article "Aztec Pleasure Gardens," Hernán Cortés described the Aztec's spectacular botanical gardens in a letter to King Charles V:

> *There are ... very refreshing gardens with many trees and sweet-scented flowers, bathing places of fresh water ... [There was also] a large orchard near the house overlooked by a high terrace with many beautiful corridors and rooms. Within the orchard is a great square pool of fresh water, very well constructed, with sides of handsome masonry, around which runs a walk with a well-laid pavement of tiles, so wide that four persons can walk abreast on it, and 400 paces square, making in all 1,600 paces. On the other side of this promenade toward the wall of the garden are hedges of latticework made of cane, behind which are all sorts of plantations of trees and aromatic herbs. The pool contains many fish and different kinds of waterfowl.*

They had also developed a scientific classification system to help them categorize plants. By using specific word parts in the plant's name, they could provide enough description to reveal details about that organism. These word parts could provide clues as to what the plant looked like, what color it was, where it grew, and what (if any) medicinal benefits it had.

For example, if a plant was classified as an herb, it would have *xihuitl* as part of its name. If that same plant grew in water, it would also contain *at(l)* in its name. If the plant produced sweet, fleshy fruits, it would contain *zapotla*.

It is important to realize how advanced this scientific naming system was for the time period. In the 1500s, the Spanish who arrived in Tenochtitlán referred to any big, colorful flower as a rose. It did not matter if the flower was indeed a rose or if it was a dahlia, a marigold, or a zinnia—all flowers with few similarities to the rose. The Aztecs, however, knew how important it was to have accuracy in their naming conventions.

CHAPTER FIVE

BY THE NUMBERS

One look at the advanced architecture and engineering projects constructed by the Aztecs and it is obvious that they must have had a highly advanced knowledge of mathematics. After all, there is really no way they could have built their impressive structures without knowing how numbers, angles, weights, and measurements worked together in a practical way.

One example of this is the arrangement of Tenochtitlán: a perfectly rectangular Sacred Precinct that extended out into four precisely measured quadrants. The buildings themselves also utilized clear aspects of geometric principles: right angles, isosceles triangles, parallel lines, circles, squares, and various types of regular polygons. It is clear that the city center—and all of the buildings—were meticulously planned and architecturally designed. A deep understanding of mathematics was required to make that happen.

GIVE ME TWENTY

The Aztecs had a specific number system that differed from the modern, widespread base-ten number system. Theirs was actually a base-twenty, or vigesimal, system. Some experts speculate that this is because they used all twenty digits (ten fingers and ten toes) to count. Others say it was used because the number twenty had religious and astronomical significance. The Aztecs had symbols that represented certain numbers, and then these symbols could be combined to form larger numbers. For instance, to describe the number thirty-one, an Aztec would write the symbol for twenty, the symbol for ten, and the symbol for one. When read, the final number to be expressed was found by adding all those symbols together.

Experts know the Aztecs used a vigesimal system because the numbers one through twenty are all represented with different symbols. Then, after twenty, those same symbols are used in combination over and over again until the next multiple of twenty is used—forty, sixty, eighty, one hundred, and so forth. All multiples of twenty get their own new symbol.

SURVEYING THE SCENE

The *Codex Vergara* and the *Santa María Asunción Codex* both provide clues to the Aztecs' knowledge and use of mathematics. These documents describe the landholdings of different parts of the Aztec Empire. In 2008, researchers uncovered some interesting information from these documents. A geographer from the University of Wisconsin—Barbara Williams—and a mathematician from Mexico—María del Carmen Jorge y Jorge—found that the drawings in these documents show the Aztecs' knowledge of addition, subtraction, multiplication, and division.

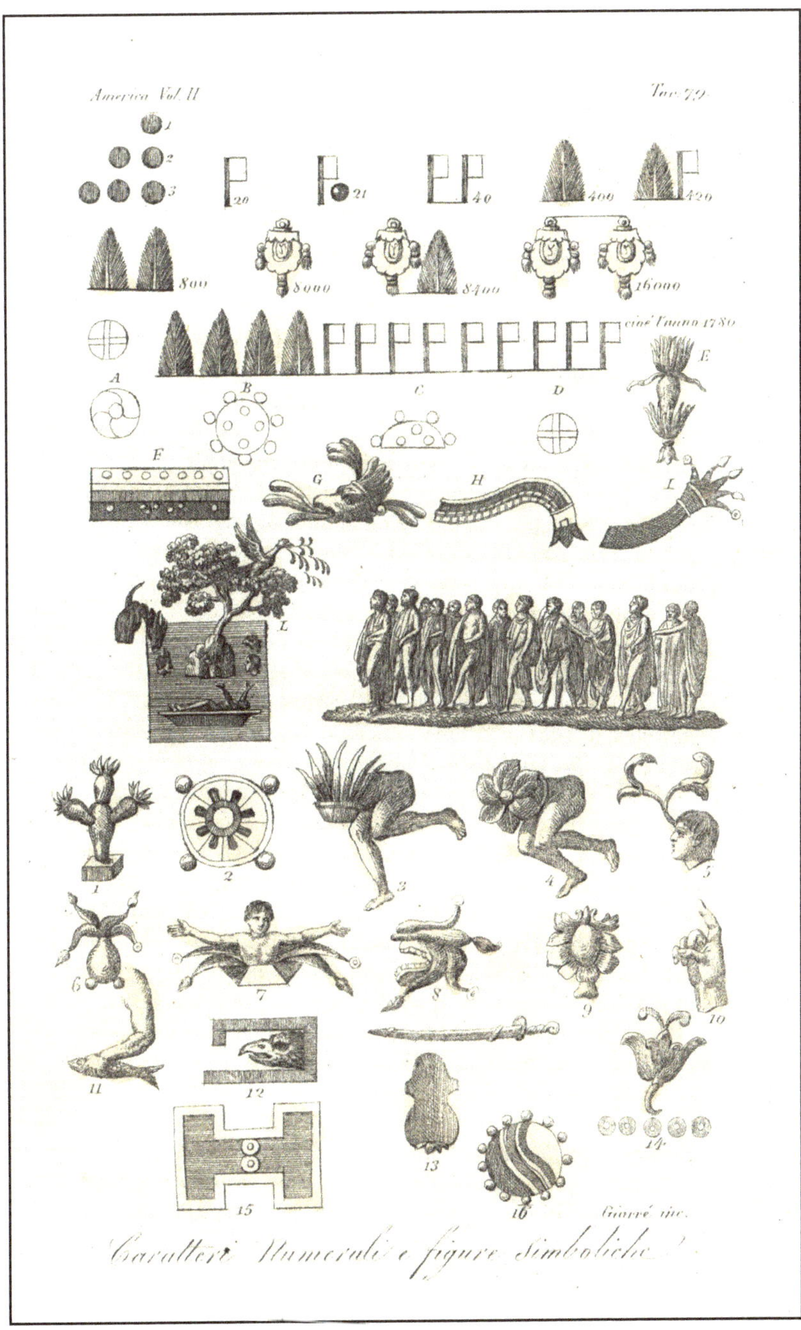

The Aztecs used symbolic characters in their artwork. This engraving includes number glyphs as well as the symbols for day, night, midnight, year, century, sky, air, earth, water, and flood.

It is apparent from these drawings that the surveyors who measured the land used several different types of problem-solving operations to calculate the perimeter and area of each parcel of land. As journalist Constance Holden explained in an article in *Science*, "Some parcels involved simply multiplying length by width. But in other, irregular four-sided lots, they had to come up with different approaches, such as multiplying the average of two opposite sides by an adjacent side." Researchers have also found that the Aztecs had unique fractional symbols used for portions of a measurement. The rod they used to measure distance was about 8.2 feet (2.5 m) long; any measurement less than one full rod was denoted by the use of such symbols as an arrow, hand, heart, or bone. "We established the proportions as: Two arrows = one land rod, five hearts = two land rods, five hands = three land rods, five bones = one land rod, and three arms = one land rod," Barbara Williams explained to Roger Highfield of *The Telegraph*.

Though this system was far from perfect, it still demonstrated a highly advanced understanding of mathematics. Unlike modern societies, the Aztecs did not have an international committee to define absolute measurements, such as the meter; they had to rely on a real, physical object that represented a unit of length. However, they understood that not every measurement could be exactly described in terms of whole sticks. The invention of symbols to make their number notation easier to read was impressive, as it made records easier to keep—and understand.

SUN STONE MATH

One artifact that has proven particularly valuable for mathematical, cultural, and artistic research is the Aztec Sun Stone, also called the Calendar Stone. This stone is 11.74 feet (3.58 m) in diameter and is about 38.5 inches (98 cm) thick. It weighs in at 25 tons (22.7 metric tons).

(continued on the next page)

The massive Aztec Sun Stone is among the most celebrated Mesoamerican discoveries. It is a clear example of the Aztecs' advanced mathematical ability.

(continued from the previous page)

The Aztec Sun Stone was uncovered in 1790, some 200 years after the destruction of Tenochtitlán. The stone itself is rich in symbolism and contains ideographs and images that represent specific aspects of Aztec beliefs and culture. However, the way the images are arranged on the stone unquestionably shows that the creators had a great knowledge of mathematics. The stone is a large circle that it is divided into various segments by concentric circles and inscribed images. Each of these concentric circles is broken into several smaller segments, and each of these segments is given equal space in the ring. To achieve this equal distribution of space, the creators must have known how to calculate the circumference of not just the entire Sun Stone, but also the circumference of each of the concentric circles onto which they carved the images.

THE ANCIENT CALENDAR

In addition to mathematics used for record keeping and land assessment, the Aztecs had a highly developed calendar system. Their calendar calculations were tied to their religious beliefs and knowledge of astronomy. Historians have learned about this system by studying the Aztec codices and the artifacts discovered in archeological digging excursions.

The Aztecs used two different calendars to mark time. The *tonalpohualli* was a calendar with 260 days. This calendar determined when sacred rituals—such as sacrifices for the gods—needed to take place. It was made up of twenty months of thirteen days. Notice the importance of the twenty months here, as it relates to the base-twenty number system used by the Aztecs. It is believed that the calendar was based on astronomical observations relating to the planet Venus's orbit in the sky.

The *xiuhpohualli* was a calendar with 365 days, similar to modern calendars. This calendar was a solar calendar and described a one-year solar cycle. It was made up of eighteen months of twenty days each. The base-twenty number system is used once again for these calculations, but this time it applied to the number of days. This calendar was used to determine when farmers should plant and harvest their crops. It also determined when particular religious festivals were held.

The calendars were used together, and every fifty-two years, a full cycle of both calendars would be completed. When this happened, the Aztecs celebrated their most important religious festival. It was called the New Fire Ceremony and included food, dancing, music, offerings, and human sacrifice. The end of each fifty-two year *xiuhmolpilli* (year bundle) was regarded with great celebration, but also with great fear. Aztec belief indicated that the

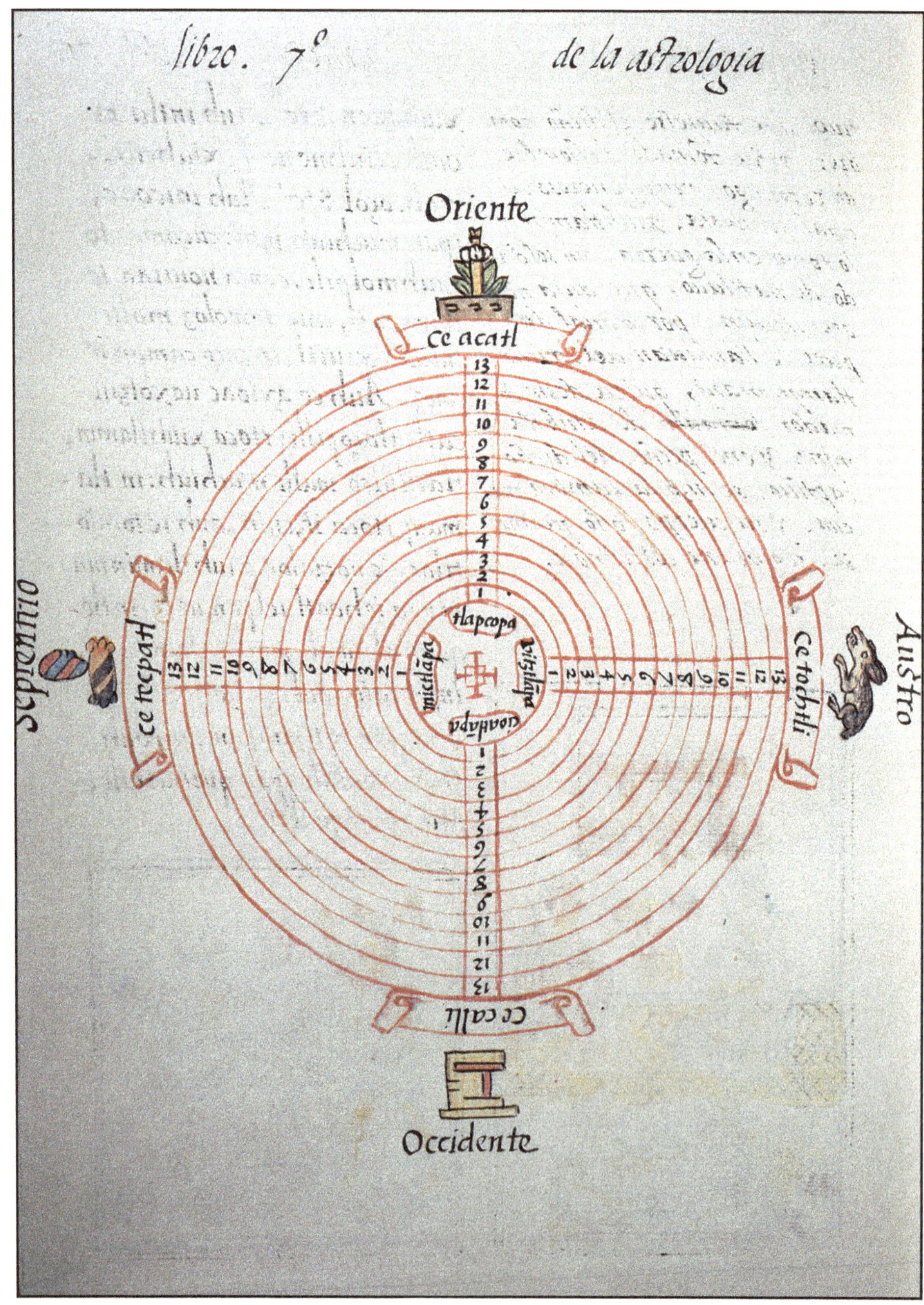

This drawing, found in the *Florentine Codex*, shows an example of a fifty-two-year xiuhmolpilli

world was in danger of being destroyed at the end of each xiuhmolpilli, and the New Fire Ceremony was a way of preventing that destruction. Because the calendar was so important to the Aztecs' religious beliefs, the calculations of each day, month, and year were extremely important. To make the most accurate predictions possible, they had to use precise mathematics.

CHAPTER SIX

GETTING THE JOB DONE

The Aztecs were accomplished in every field. The citizens who worked as farmers, engineers, builders, merchants, artists, scientists, priests, painters, stonecutters, craftsmen, and warriors each had a specific set of skills to master their craft. Along with these skills came an equally specific—and equally important—set of tools. To achieve their diverse ambitions, the Aztecs understood the importance of making efficient and effective tools to help workers do their jobs better, faster, and easier.

A SHINY STONE

One important category of tool utilized by many Aztec professions was stone tools. The Aztecs preferred one stone in particular: the shiny black rock called obsidian. This rock is a naturally occurring material that is created during volcanic eruptions. The Valley of Mexico, in which rested the heart of Aztec society, is surrounded by volcanoes, and this stone was found in abundance all around major cities. In fact, even in modern times, Mesoamerica still has the largest deposits of obsidian in the world. It makes sense, then, that the Aztecs would have figured out ways to

Obsidian was highly prized by ancient peoples in the Americas for its incredible sharpness; modern-day metal blades do not even come close.

take advantage of this common—and very useful—natural resource.

Obsidian is an extremely strong stone and it is used to make sharp objects, such as knives, arrowheads, blades, spears, and swords. It was used for domestic cooking, craft production, hunting, warfare, and ritual. Blades made from obsidian are actually much sharper than the same types of objects made out of metal. Since obsidian also shares many properties with other kinds of glass, it can be polished to use for mirrors and jewelry as well.

STONE AND SURGERY

Adrien Hannus is an anthropologist specializing in the history of American peoples. In a video for the Public Broadcasting Service (PBS), he explained how incredible the obsidian blades of the Aztecs remain, even by modern standards. Obsidian edged tools are so effective, in fact, that he encouraged his doctor to use a set of obsidian scalpels during a surgical procedure.

The doctor was impressed with how smoothly the blades worked in comparison to similar instruments made with steel blades. Hannus explained why and how these tools were more effective than their steel counterparts: under extreme magnification, the steel blade of a standard scalpel "looks like a rusty saw blade," while the obsidian blade is only a molecule thick and extends in a "straight line." For precise cutting, it is obvious that a straight edge is more effective than a saw. Further research with stone tools for surgery has shown that obsidian can "produce cutting edges many times finer than even the best steel scalpels," according to an article by Peter Shadbolt for CNN. Shadbolt interviewed Lee Green of Alberta, Canada, who claimed that he frequently uses obsidian blades in his medical practice. "The biggest advantage with obsidian is that it is the sharpest edge there is, it causes very little trauma to tissue, it heals faster, and more importantly, it heals with less scarring."

The widespread use of metal—especially steel—is often considered an important turning point in a society, particular in European history. Mass production of metal tools and weapons is nearly always accompanied by advances in other aspects of a civilization's history because of the sheer usefulness of the material. However, the Aztecs exhibited many STEM-related advances even without the introduction of iron and steel, and that is largely because of the efficiency and effectiveness of working with obsidian. Innovation typically occurs in order to fulfill a need—and if the Aztecs were doing great work with their obsidian products, no one felt the need to look for new materials, which would likely have been inferior.

ON THE BATTLEFIELD

The Aztecs were often fighting battles with neighboring peoples to secure more land and acquire more subjects. The soldiers used all kinds of weaponry—most of which involved some kind of obsidian blade. They also wore unusual clothing for battle, including feathered costumes that looked like different types of ferocious-looking animals with matching shields decorated with precious stones and feathers.

Archaeologist Frances Berdan once questioned how the artisans who made such objects were able to attach the feathers and stones to these surfaces. What kinds of adhesives did the Aztecs use to make sure their highly decorated tools and weapons were ready for war? After conducting a variety of chemical

This ceramic figure depicts an Aztec warrior in full eagle costume. It was created by an Aztec artist sometime between 1300 and 1521 CE. The piece is found at the Templo Mayor Museum in Mexico City.

research, her team was able to pinpoint the type of ingredients in this century-old glue. The Aztecs mixed a combination of natural components together to make an extremely strong adhesive—capable of holding their decorated armor together. They used resin from the copal and pine trees, combined with either beeswax or the powder from pulverized orchid bulbs.

Many of the soldiers also wore padded armor called *ichcahuipilli* cuirasses. These were protective vests made out of multiple layers of cotton. These cuirasses had a similar purpose to modern bulletproof vests. The ichcahuipilli armor could not stop bullets, of course, but it was effective at protecting individuals from being slashed by the extremely sharp obsidian weapons of the time. Historians have long known that the Aztecs used these vests based on illustrations found in one of the Aztec codices. While the inventor of the ichcahuipilli armor is unknown, there is no doubt that he or she was a STEM genius. Because Aztec society was not built around metal—unlike many contemporary civilizations—it never developed metal-based armor. However, soldiers still needed a way to protect themselves, especially since obsidian weapons were so effective. Instead of advancing military protection from leather to metal, Aztec engineers and scientists instead focused on thick padding that could stop the blades and ranged weapons of their Mesoamerican enemies.

TRICKS OF THE TRADE

Outside of warfare and weapons, the Aztecs also developed many techniques and tools for domestic life. Many of the buildings and streets of Tenochtitlán had a gleaming white appearance. Most of the city took on that appearance due to the process of plaster whitewashing. The Aztecs made their plaster by first crushing limestone and then mixing it with a recipe of sand and water. This formula, despite not having a lot of ingredients, needed to be followed exactly by engineers. If not, the plaster would not adhere or dry properly, thus rendering the mixture worthless. A lot of the city was constructed out of a stone called tezontle, which was readily available stone in the area. This is a porous volcanic stone that is rust red in color—hence the desire for whitewashing to make the city look cleaner. Masons would have either applied the whitewash with some kind of brush made out of animal hairs or a stick and cloth apparatus that would soak up enough of the solution so it could be applied to the structure. Both of these highly specialized tools would have required years of development. Masons also had to be highly skilled at their job since they needed to apply the plaster in such a way as to not leave any holes or rough and uneven surfaces on the building they were whitewashing.

Stonemasons were not in charge of plastering surfaces, but rather tasked with the responsibility of building structures out of stone, carving reliefs, making arches, and designing windows, roofs, and solid foundations. To complete their jobs, they would have needed to have access to such tools as chisels, hammers, and wedges. Though these tools have been common to all ancient societies, the Aztecs also made use of unconventional work practices. Cords and strings, for example, were also used to cut smaller stones. Stonemasons and jewelers would soak a cord or string in an abrasive. Then, they would move the wet filament back and forth over a block of stone; eventually, the string would cut through the stone.

CHAPTER SEVEN

SPANISH INVASION

Upon arriving in the land of the Aztecs, Cortés and his men marveled at what they saw. Cortés's men often referred to Tenochtitlán as the Venice of the New World. When they met ruler Montezuma II for the first time on one of the causeways that entered the city in the fall of 1519, they were presented with gifts: a gold disc of the sun, a silver disc of the moon, and his own headdress, made out of the green feathers from the quetzal, a native bird. Montezuma II wanted to impress these foreign warriors. He thought that they were the divine emissaries of the god Quetzalcoatl who—according to Aztec legend—had promised he would someday return from the east. The Aztec leader invited them to enter the city and stay as special guests in one of his palaces.

THEY CAME TO CONQUER

However, the Spanish were not in the New World just to visit the Aztecs and bid them good tidings. They were conquistadores—conquerors. Their intent was to seize control of the empire in the name of their monarch, the king of Spain. After arriving, Cortés

Montezuma II, shown here in full regalia, was the last emperor of the Aztecs. He died in Spanish captivity in 1520 as part of Cortés's conquest.

immediately started plotting. He and his men took Montezuma II hostage and took control of the city for many months.

In the spring of 1520, Cortés and a small group of his men left Tenochtitlán to go fight a battle with a Spanish force that had just arrived from Cuba. When he returned, the city was facing a rebellion by the Aztec population, who did not want to be under Spanish rule. Cortés and his men fled the city, but many of the Spanish soldiers drowned in the lake when their vessel—stuffed with Aztec riches—sunk. Montezuma II was killed during the fighting, either by the Spanish or the insurgent Aztecs. His brother, Cuitlahuac, became the next king.

Cortés then enlisted the help of some of the neighboring tribes and returned to Tenochtitlán. He laid siege to the city for months. The Spanish and their allies cut off all supplies and water into the city; they blocked the causeways; halted any transport by canoe; and even seized control of the aqueduct. The Aztecs fought to the very end—but on August 13, 1521, they were forced to surrender. Historical records do not provide a clear estimate of the losses, but researchers believe that anywhere from tens to hundreds of thousands of Aztecs died during the siege and in the subsequent months, thanks to diseases brought by the Spanish, such as smallpox.

The Spanish razed much of the city to build their own capital of New Spain. They called it Mexico City—a tribute to the Aztecs, considering the original people called themselves the Mexicas. The Spanish

After the Spanish captured Tenochtitlán, they demolished the city. Then, they built Mexico City in its place. Some of the stones from the Aztec structures were used in the new Spanish edifices.

demolished the king's palace, the Templo Mayor, and other large structures and used the stones to build cathedrals, the national palace, and other colonial buildings in the style of their own traditional Spanish architecture. Over time, the Spanish also drained the lakes so more of the land could be used for building projects and farmland.

TEMPLO MAYOR MUSEUM

Visitors to Mexico City can spend time at the Templo Mayor Museum, located in the center of the city. The museum includes an actual archaeological dig site, where visitors come face to face with the long-lost city of the Aztecs. Tourists can see part of the pyramid's twin staircases and the seven different layers of the structure that were built over generations. There is even a stone wall with a rack of human skulls—likely the victims of the Aztecs' sacrifices to their gods.

The Templo Mayor Museum features some breathtaking exhibits, including a glimpse of the ruins of Tenochtitlán, shown here.

In addition to the archaeological site, there is an indoor museum with eight exhibit halls that house some of the most important relics that have been uncovered at the site over the decades. The Coyolxauhqui monolith is there, as is the famous Aztec Sun Stone. Both are displayed vertically on the wall, even though the Aztecs would have placed them horizontally on the ground when they were actually in use. In addition, there are a number of other artifacts that reveal details about Aztec life in the capital city, including obsidian knives, rubber balls, jade and turquoise masks, colorfully painted tiles, various relief artwork, sculptures, and ritual or religious objects.

AZTECS LEFT THEIR MARK

Just as Tenochtitlán was the most populated city in the Americas during the sixteenth century, Mexico City is today one of the largest cities and most populated metropolises in the Western Hemisphere. More than 8.8 million people live in the city. About 1.5 million descendants of the Aztecs still live in Mexico City and rural areas of Mexico. Many speak their native language, Nahuatl. Many Nahuatl words have even made it into English, such as avocado, guacamole, cacao and chocolate, mole, chili, chia, coyote, and tomato. The Aztecs left a significant mark on the New World. Through their impressive engineering and architectural projects, they were able to build one of the largest civilizations of precolonial America. They showed that it is possible to tame the land, harness the elements, and make the seemingly impossible a reality by utilizing advanced knowledge in science, technology, mathematics, and engineering. After studying their many achievements, it is no wonder that some experts today believe that the Aztecs were arguably the greatest engineers of the Americas. As more and more archaeological evidence is uncovered in future generations, that belief will become even more rooted in the historical record.

TIMELINE

1325 Tenochtitlán is founded.

1350 Causeway construction to connect Tenochtitlán to the mainland is started.

1370 Tenoch, the Aztecs' religious ruler, dies.

1376 Acamapichtli becomes the first Aztec king.

1390 Construction begins on the first version of the Templo Mayor.

1395 Acamapichtli dies and Huitzilihuitl becomes king.

1417 Huitzilihuitl dies and Chimalpopoca becomes king.

1418 The first aqueduct is built.

1427 Chimalpopoca dies and Itzcoatl becomes king.

1440 Itzcoatl dies and Montezuma I becomes king.

1449 Tenochtitlán is severely damaged by flooding and the original aqueduct is destroyed. Construction of the second aqueduct begins shortly after.

1469 Montezuma I dies and Azayactl becomes king.

1481 Azayactl dies and Tizoc becomes king.

1486 Tizoc dies and Ahuitzotl becomes king.

1502 Ahuitzotl dies and Montezuma II becomes king.

1519 Cortés lands on the Yucatán Peninsula, burns his ships to show that he is intending to stay and conquer. He arrives in Tenochtitlán on November 8 and seizes control of the city after taking Montezuma II hostage.

1520 Residents of Tenochtitlán revolt. Montezuma II is killed at the hands of the Spaniards or his own people. His brother, Cuitlahuac, becomes king.

1521 Cuitlahuac surrenders to Cortés after a several-month siege of the city. He is eventually executed by the Spanish. The Aztec Empire officially ends. Spanish conquistadores raze the city of Tenochtitlán, which is later rebuilt in Spanish colonial style.

GLOSSARY

aqueduct A manmade channel that is meant to allow water to flow from the source to a different location.

causeways Roads that have been built at a slightly higher elevation than the ground or water that surround them.

codices Manuscripts that are compiled into a book form.

concentric Describing circles of various circumferences that share the same center and overlap.

conquistadores People who conquer other people. This word is especially used with the Spanish and Portuguese who conquered the Americas in the fifteenth and sixteenth centuries.

dike A long wall or buildup of earth that is built along a body of water to prevent flooding.

drawbridges Bridges that have sections that can raise and lower to allow shipping traffic to pass from one part of the water to another.

emissaries Representatives sent on a special mission by another.

ensign A flag, pennant, or banner.

ideographs Pictures that represents specific words, phrases, or ideas.

Mesoamerica A region in Central America where many pre-Columbian societies flourished. The countries of Mexico, Belize, Guatemala, El Salvador, Honduras, Nicaragua, and Costa Rica are part of this region.

monolith A large block of stone that has been shaped or carved to make a monument of some kind.

piling A length of wood (or steel, concrete, or stone) that is pounded into the ground to provide structural support for anything built or placed above it.

public works Government projects that build such things as roads, utilities (water, sewer, electricity) for a community.

quarries Places from which large pieces of stone or smaller bits of rock are cut and harvested for use in building projects elsewhere.

quetzal A species of blue green bird in the Americas that was highly valued for its beautiful feathers used by the Mesoamerican kings.

sluice gates A sliding structure on a dike or dam that allows water to flow from one side of the wall to the other.

tezontle Rust-red stone found near Tenochtitlán that was used to build many of the city's grand monuments; a porous volcanic stone.

tributes Taxes, in the form of money or goods, that subjects must pay to an overlord or ruling kingdom.

vigesimal A number system that is based on groups of twenty.

ziggurats Constructions, similar to pyramids, with flat tops.

FOR MORE INFORMATION

American Anthropological Association (AAA)
2300 Clarendon Boulevard, Suite 1301
Arlington, VA 22201
(703) 528-1902
Website: https://www.americananthro.org
Facebook: @AmericanAnthropologicalAssociation
Instagram and Twitter: @AmericanAnthro
Founded in 1902, this nonprofit organization based in the Washington, DC, area is the world's largest association of professional anthropologists. The AAA publishes more than twenty journals and offers career and professional development services, provides scholarships for university students, and hosts research conferences twice a year.

Archaeological Institute of America
44 Beacon Street
Boston, MA 02108
(857) 305-9350
Website: https://www.archaeological.org
Facebook: @Archaeological.Institute
Instagram and Twitter: @archaeology_aia
Founded in 1879, this nonprofit is the oldest and largest archaeological society in North America. Its membership—which exceeds 210,000—includes students, professionals, and those sharing a passion for the ancient world. Led by a staff of professionals and volunteers, the organization promotes public understanding in the field of archaeology by supporting professional research

projects and sharing new discoveries in its *Archaeology* magazine.

Mexicolore
28 Warriner Gardens
London SW11 4EB
United Kingdom
(44) 20 7622 9577
Website: http://www.mexicolore.co.uk
Twitter: @Mexicolore
Mexicolore was founded in 1980 by Graciela Sánchez and Ian Mursell. The aim of the organization is to educate the community on all aspects of Mexican culture, specifically the Aztec and Mayan civilizations. The website features many articles by experts, and the team also travels to schools and museums to provide informative presentations.

National Institute of Anthropology and History
8 Seminario Street
Cuahtemoc, D.F., 06060
Mexico
(55) 4166 0780, ext. 412930 or 412933
Website: https://www.templomayor.inah.gob.mx/english
Facebook, Instagram, and Twitter: @INAHmx
This archaeological society is dedicated to uncovering Aztec ruins from the past at the Templo Mayor site and other areas of Mexico City. It is also responsible for protecting and securing historic

monuments and archaeological sites throughout the country. The museum at the Templo Mayor site offers opportunities for students, adults, and tourists to learn more about the Aztec civilization through exhibits and access to the dig site.

Peabody Museum of Archaeology & Ethnology
Administrative Offices
11 Divinity Avenue
Cambridge, MA 02138
(617) 496-1638
Website: https://www.peabody.harvard.edu
Facebook and Twitter: @PeabodyMuseum
As one of the oldest archaeological museums in the world, the Peabody at Harvard houses a variety of artifacts and art from various world cultures, with an emphasis on those that were native to the Americas. Through the exhibits, workshops, and lectures, visitors are able to gain a better appreciation for the ancient world and human cultural history.

Society for American Archaeology
1111 14th Street NW, Suite 800
Washington, DC 20005-5622
(202) 789-8200
Website: https://www.saa.org
Facebook: @SAAorgfb
Instagram: @societyforamaricanarchaeology
Twitter: @SAAorg

This organization's mission is to help the general public gain a better understanding of and appreciation for humanity's past. The group promotes research, encourages the investigation into archaeological records, works to protect artifacts and dig sites, offers educational opportunities for the public, and publishes research findings.

FOR FURTHER READING

Aguilar-Moreno, Manuel. *Handbook to Life in the Aztec World*. New York, NY: Oxford University Press, 2006.

Apte, Sunita. *The Aztec Empire*. New York, NY: Scholastic, 2010.

Baquedano, Elizabeth. *Aztec, Inca & Maya: Discover the World of the Aztecs, Incas, and Mayas—Their Beliefs, Rituals, and Civilizations*. New York, NY: Dorling Kindersley Limited, 2011.

Berdan, Frances. *Aztec Archaeology and Ethnohistory*. Cambridge, UK: Cambridge University Press, 2014.

León-Portilla, Miguel. *Fifteen Poets of the Aztec World*. Norman, OK: University of Oklahoma Press, 2017.

Levy, Buddy. *Conquistador: Hernán Cortés, King Montezuma, and the Last Stand of the Aztecs*. New York, NY: Bantam Books, 2008.

Long, Erin. *Aztec*. New York, NY: PowerKids Press, 2016.

Mundy, Barbara E. *The Death of Aztec Tenochtitlan, the Life of Mexico City*. Austin, TX: University of Texas Press Austin, 2015.

Phillips, Charles. *The Complete Illustrated History of the Aztec & Maya: The Definitive Chronicle of the Ancient Peoples of Central America and Mexico Including the Aztec, Maya, Olmec, Mixtec, Toltec, and Zapotec*. Irvine, CA: Hermes House, 2015.

Siepel, Kevin H. *Conquistador Voices: The Spanish Conquest of the Americas as Recounted Largely by the Participants*. Angola, NY: Spruce Tree Press, 2015.

BIBLIOGRAPHY

Aguilar-Moreno, Manuel. "Aztec Art & Architecture." FAMSI. Retrieved February 25, 2019. http://www.famsi.org/research/aguilar/index.html.

Ashenburg, Katherine. "Clean Aztecs, Dirty Spaniards." Mexicolore. Retrieved January 31, 2019. http://www.mexicolore.co.uk/aztecs/home/clean-aztecs-dirty-spaniards.

Berdan, Frances. *Aztec Archaeology and Ethnohistory.* Cambridge, UK: Cambridge University Press, 2014.

Conway, Richard. "Rural Indians and Technological Innovation, from the Chinampas of Xochimilco and Beyond." *Oxford Research Encyclopedias*, February 2018. http://oxfordre.com/latinamericanhistory/view/10.1093/acrefore/9780199366439.001.0001/acrefore-9780199366439-e-530.

De Tovar, Juan. "The Eagle, the Snake, and the Cactus in the Founding of Tenochtitlan." World Digital Library. Retrieved February 1, 2019. https://www.wdl.org/en/item/6749.

Flood, Julia. "Aztec Transport." Mexicolore. Retrieved January 29, 2019. http://www.mexicolore.co.uk/aztecs/kids/aztec-transport.

Helmke_Library. "Reconstructing Ancient Aztec Superglue—Frances Berdan." YouTube, March 14, 2012. https://www.youtube.com/watch?v=DhnznaM7l0c.

Highfield, Roger. "How the Aztecs Could Count Hand on Heart." *Telegraph*, April 3, 2008. https://www.telegraph.co.uk.

Holden, Constance. "How Aztecs Did the Math." *Science*, April 3, 2008. https://www

.sciencemag.org/news/2008/04/how-aztecs-did-math?r3f_986=http://www.google.com.

Kaufman, Rachel. "Aztec, Maya Were Rubber-Making Masters?" *National Geographic*, June 30, 2010. https://news.nationalgeographic.com/news/2010/06/100628-science-ancient-maya-aztec-rubber-balls-beheaded.

MGH. "Aztecs Chinampas." YouTube, August 4, 2011. https://www.youtube.com/watch?v=hew9ZDO1caw.

Mundy, Barbara. "Water and the Aztec Landscape in the Valley of Mexico" Mexicolore. Retrieved February 1, 2019. http://www.mexicolore.co.uk/aztecs/home/water-in-valley-of-mexico.

Mursell, Ian. "Aztec Pleasure Gardens." Mexicolore. Retrieved January 15, 2019. http://www.mexicolore.co.uk/aztecs/aztefacts/aztec-pleasure-gardens.

Mursell, Ian. "The Eagle and the Snake." Mexicolore. Retrieved February 1, 2019. http://www.mexicolore.co.uk/aztecs/ask-us/eagle-and-the-snake.

Mursell, Ian. "King Canoe." Mexicolore. Retrieved February 1, 2019. http://www.mexicolore.co.uk/aztecs/aztec-life/king-canoe.

Ortiz-Franco, Luis. "The Aztec Number System, Algebra, and Ethnomathematics." In *Perspectives on Indigenous Peoples of North America*, Elaine Hankes and Gerald R. Fast, eds. National Council of Teachers of Mathematics: Reston, VA, 2002.

PBS. "Dr. Adrien Hannus: Stone Blade Surgery." PBS. Retrieved February 2, 2019. http://www.pbs.org/time-team/experience-archaeology/stone-blade-surgery.

Riding, Alan. "Discovery of Aztec Monolith in Mexico City Sparks a Major Excavation." *New York Times*, December 10, 1978. https://www.nytimes.com/1978/12/10/archives/discovery-of-aztec-monolith-in-mexico-city-sparls-a-major.html.

Shadbolt, Peter. "How Stone Age Blades are Still Cutting It in Modern Surgery." CNN, April 2, 2015. https://www.cnn.com/2015/04/02/health/surgery-scalpels-obsidian/index.html.

Smith, Michael E. "Life in the Provinces of the Aztec Empire." *Scientific American*, January 1, 2005. https://www.scientificamerican.com/article/life-in-the-provinces-of-the-aztec-2005-01.

Summerson, Terrance. "Some Thoughts on the Design of the Aztec Sun Stone." Mexicolore. Retrieved January 22, 2019. http://www.mexicolore.co.uk/aztecs/you-contribute/th-design-of-the-aztec-sunstone.

INDEX

M

N

O

P

Q

R

S

T

V

W

X

Z

ABOUT THE AUTHOR

Amie Jane Leavitt graduated from Brigham Young University and is an accomplished author, researcher, and photographer. She has written numerous books for young readers, has contributed to online and print media, and has worked as a consultant, writer, and editor for educational publishing and assessment companies.

PHOTO CREDITS

Cover Richard I'Anson/Lonely Planet Images/Getty Images; pp. 5, 9, 27, 45 DEA/G. Dagli Orti/De Agostini /Getty Images; pp. 11, 48 De Agostini Picture Library /Getty Images; p. 13 James Barber/Corbis/Getty Images; p. 18 Edward E. Ayer Digital Collection, Newberry Library. Ayer 655.51 .C8 1524b; p. 22 Private Collection/Look and Learn/Elgar Collection/Bridgeman Images; p. 30 Dorling Kindersley/Getty Images; p. 35 NiceImages /Shutterstock.com; p. 37 DEA/G. Sioen/De Agostini /Getty Images; p. 43 Florilegius/SSPL/Getty Images; p. 51 Werner Forman/Universal Images Group/Getty Images; p. 54 Jean-Pierre Courau/Gamma-Rapho/Getty Images; p. 59 Heritage Images/Hulton Archive/Getty Images; p. 61 Lanmas/Alamy Stock Photo; p. 62 Ronaldo Schemidt/AFP/Getty Images; cover and interior pages (dark textured background) Midiwaves/Shutterstock.com; interior pages (scroll pattern page borders) Megin /Shutterstock.com, (yellow marbled page borders) Chizhovao/Shutterstock.com.

Design and Layout: Nicole Russo-Duca; Editor: Siyavush Saidian; Photo Researcher: Cindy Reiman